BIOGRAPHY FROM
ANCIENT CIVILIZATIONS
LEGENDS, FOLKLORE, AND STORIES OF ANCIENT WORLDS

The Life and Times of

ARISTOTLE

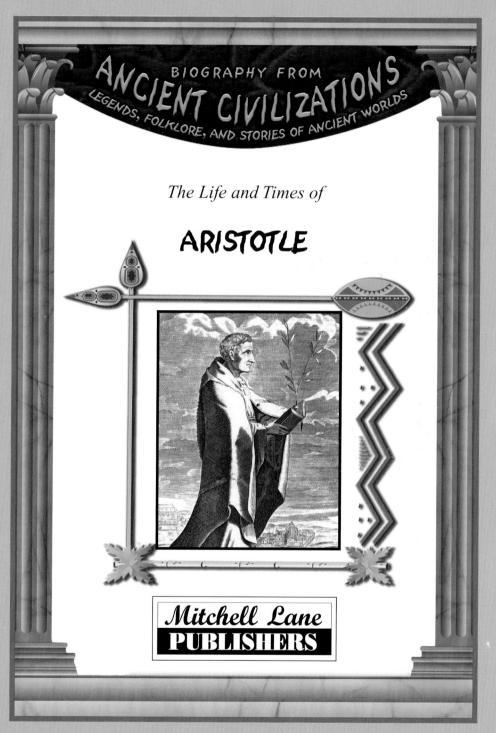

Mitchell Lane
PUBLISHERS

P.O. Box 196
Hockessin, Delaware 19707

BIOGRAPHY FROM
ANCIENT CIVILIZATIONS
LEGENDS, FOLKLORE, AND STORIES OF ANCIENT WORLDS

Titles
in the Series

The Life and Times of

Alexander the Great	Herodotus
Archimedes	Hippocrates
Aristotle	Homer
Augustus Caesar	Joan of Arc
Buddha	Julius Caesar
Catherine the Great	King Arthur
Charlemagne	Marco Polo
Cicero	Moses
Cleopatra	Nero
Confucius	Pericles
Constantine	Plato
Genghis Khan	Rameses the Great
Hammurabi	Socrates

BIOGRAPHY FROM

ANCIENT CIVILIZATIONS
LEGENDS, FOLKLORE, AND STORIES OF ANCIENT WORLDS

The Life and Times of

ARISTOTLE

Jim Whiting

Printing   1   2   3   4   5   6   7   8   9

Library of Congress Cataloging-in-Publication Data

Whiting, Jim, 1943-
    The life and times of Aristotle / by Jim Whiting.
        p. cm. — (Biography from ancient civilizations)
    Includes bibliographical references and index.
    ISBN 1-58415-508-6 (library bound)
    1. Aristotle—Juvenile literature. 2. Philosophers—Greece—Biography—Juvenile literature. 3. Greece—History—To 146 B.C.—Juvenile literature. I. Title. II. Series.
B481.W45 2006
185—dc22   2005036695

ISBN-10: 1-58415-508-6   ISBN-13: 978-1-58415-508-9

ABOUT THE AUTHOR: Jim Whiting has been a remarkably versatile and accomplished journalist, writer, editor, and photographer for more than 30 years. A voracious reader since early childhood, Mr. Whiting has written and edited about 200 nonfiction children's books. His subjects range from authors to zoologists and include contemporary pop icons and classical musicians, saints and scientists, emperors and explorers. Representative titles include *The Life and Times of Franz Liszt, The Life and Times of Julius Caesar, Charles Schulz, Charles Darwin and the Origin of the Species,* and *Juan Ponce de Leon.*

Other career highlights are a lengthy stint publishing Northwest Runner, the first piece of original fiction to appear in *Runners World* magazine, hundreds of descriptions and venue photographs for America Online, e-commerce product writing, sports editor for the *Bainbridge Island Review,* light verse in a number of magazines, and acting as the official photographer for the Antarctica Marathon.

He lives in Washington State with his wife and two teenage sons.

PHOTO CREDITS: Cover, pp. 1, 3—Science Photo Library/Photo Researchers; p. 6—Erlangen; p. 8—MPI/Getty; pp. 10, 22, 26, 39—Hulton Archive/Getty Images; p. 12—Sharon Beck; p. 25—Metropolitan Museum of Art; p. 28—Superstock; p. 36—Jamie Kondrchek; p. 41—Getty Images.

PUBLISHER'S NOTE: This story is based on the author's extensive research, which he believes to be accurate. Documentation of such research is contained on page 47.

The internet sites referenced herein were active as of the publication date. Due to the fleeting nature of some web sites, we cannot guarantee they will all be active when you are reading this book.

To reflect current usage, we have chosen to use the secular era designations BCE ("before the common era") and CE ("of the common era") instead of the traditional designations BC ("before Christ") and AD (*anno Domini,* "in the year of the Lord").

BIOGRAPHY FROM ANCIENT CIVILIZATIONS

LEGENDS, FOLKLORE, AND STORIES OF ANCIENT WORLDS

The Life and Times of

ARISTOTLE

*For Your Information

This bust of Aristotle was probably carved during his lifetime. The artist would have painted his eyes to make the figure seem more lifelike. Over the centuries the paint has disappeared.

CHAPTER
ONE

WHO'S THE SMARTEST OF THEM ALL?

Who's the most intelligent person who ever lived?

Of course, there is no absolute answer. Human history is filled with many brilliant people, and not everyone would vote for the same person. However, a few names seem to be mentioned much more frequently than others when this question is asked.

Perhaps the most common answer is Albert Einstein. As the year 1905 dawned, almost no one had heard of him. He had been a poor student. He worked at a low-paying, menial job. By the end of the year, he had published several scientific papers that he had worked on in his spare time. These papers made him world famous. One of them contained the revolutionary equation $E = mc^2$, the foundation of Einstein's theory of relativity. The equation shows that physical matter and energy are one and the same. An essential element in modern-day science, it changed the way people understood the world. After his theories became accepted, people gave the nickname "Einstein" to anyone who seemed especially bright.

Because of how women in most societies were treated before the twentieth century, the brilliance of most women has not been recorded. We may never know the names of women who could

Albert Einstein is one of the most famous scientists who ever lived. His outstanding accomplishments earned him the Nobel Prize in Physics in 1921.

have been standouts. Besides Einstein, some candidates for "smartest man" follow:

- William Shakespeare. Many people consider him to be the greatest writer of all time.
- Leonardo da Vinci. He painted *Mona Lisa* and *The Last Supper,* two of the world's most famous works of art. He also sketched plans for mechanical devices that others wouldn't understand for hundreds of years.
- Thomas Jefferson. One of the most gifted politicians in U.S. history, he drafted the Declaration of Independence.
- Benjamin Franklin. Franklin was also a gifted politician and an outstanding writer, especially noted for his sly sense of humor. A daring scientist as well, he proved that lightning is a form of electricity.
- Confucius. A Chinese teacher and philosopher who lived 500 years before Jesus, he became the most respected mind in Chinese history.

- Dante Alighieri. This Italian poet wrote the *Divine Comedy* in the early 1300s. It is considered a classic of world literature.

Dante had someone else in mind. He referred to his choice as *il maestro di color che sanno*. That phrase is translated as "the master of those who know."[1]

Dante's candidate was Aristotle.

Aristotle was a philosopher who lived nearly 2,400 years ago in ancient Greece, where philosophy was extremely important. *Philosophy* comes from two words that mean "love of wisdom." The Greeks, who were very curious, used philosophy to study people and everything else in the world.

Philosophy has applications in nearly every area of life, including politics. "For centuries, [philosophers'] duties included advising rulers how to govern wisely, and subjects when (and when not) to obey,"[2] notes professor Richard E. Rubenstein. In fact, philosophy in Greece should have come with a warning label: "Caution—may be hazardous to your health." Socrates, one of the most renowned ancient philosophers, was executed for his beliefs. Plato, his most famous student, nearly suffered the same fate. So did Aristotle.

Aristotle grew up in a world in which people believed in a whole group of gods, and that these gods were responsible for nearly everything that happened. Aristotle came to have a different belief. He wanted to understand the natural causes of events.

Unlike many thinkers, he wasn't afraid to get dirty. One of his favorite places for research was a tide pool. He would wade in water up to his waist, observing sea creatures in their natural habitat.

Until a couple of centuries ago, Aristotle was considered the world's greatest scientist. His views on the natural world went practically unchallenged for many centuries. He also influenced other areas of thinking. The U.S. Constitution has his fingerprints all over it. Many movie producers consider his book *The Poetics* to be the "bible of

Aristotle (left) is especially famous for serving as the tutor for Alexander the Great when Alexander was a teenager.

screenwriting." He tutored Alexander the Great, whom many people consider to be the world's greatest conqueror. He established the Lyceum, one of the most prestigious schools of the ancient world.

Twentieth-century philosopher Gilbert Ryle calls Aristotle "the one all-around genius in human history."[3] Scholar Jonathan Barnes agrees. "Choose a field of research, and Aristotle laboured in it; pick a field of human endeavour, and Aristotle discoursed about it. His range is astonishing."[4]

Some of the topics he examined illustrate this range. Justice. Politics. Poetry. The best way to live. The pursuit of pleasure. Public speaking. Plants. Animals. Magnets. Motion. Astronomy. Dissection. The Nile River. He even wrote a definitive list of winners of the Olympic Games and other ancient athletic contests.

Yet Aristotle and his accumulated wisdom nearly vanished after his death. The story of his writings' recovery and recirculation is full of adventure.

Aristotle and the Movies

Plutarch, an ancient historian, sneered that Aristotle's books "are written in a style which makes them useless for ordinary teaching."[5] Many people would disagree. These people include prominent Hollywood filmmakers. Gary Ross, who wrote the script for and directed the 2003 hit movie *Seabiscuit*, says that Aristotle's *Poetics* "is the best book on screenwriting."[6] Screenwriter and director Michael Tierno adds, "The criteria Hollywood executives use to evaluate screenplays are exactly those the legendary philosopher thought were the nuts and bolts of ancient drama more than 2,000 years ago."[7]

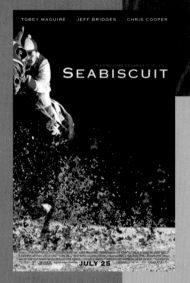

TOBEY MAGUIRE   JEFF BRIDGES   CHRIS COOPER

SEABISCUIT

JULY 25

According to Aristotle, there are six of these "nuts and bolts." One is plot, the way in which the incidents in the drama are put together. Second is character, the different personal qualities that the actors demonstrate. Third is thought, in which a general truth is revealed. Fourth is diction, the way in which an actor speaks his or her lines. Closely related is song, the fifth. "Song" doesn't necessarily mean that an actor sings the lines of the play. It refers to the rhythm of the words. Finally, a play needs spectacular equipment, or what we might call special effects.

There are other important aspects to drama. Every movie or play must be unified. It has to have a beginning, a middle, and an end. Most films do begin at the beginning of the story. Some start in the middle, and flashbacks reveal the beginning. This "back story" gives meaning to the action.

Another important factor is what Aristotle terms *mimesis*, or imitation. Most characters in a drama exhibit qualities that we should emulate, or imitate. Other characters may be "low-lifes." They demonstrate qualities we should avoid.

Another ingredient comes as the hero faces a problem that puts him or her in a tight spot. We feel pity for the person undergoing the difficulty. We also feel terror as we imagine the same thing happening to us. But we realize that what we are seeing is not real. As a result, we feel a catharsis. We are cleansed and inspired emotionally.

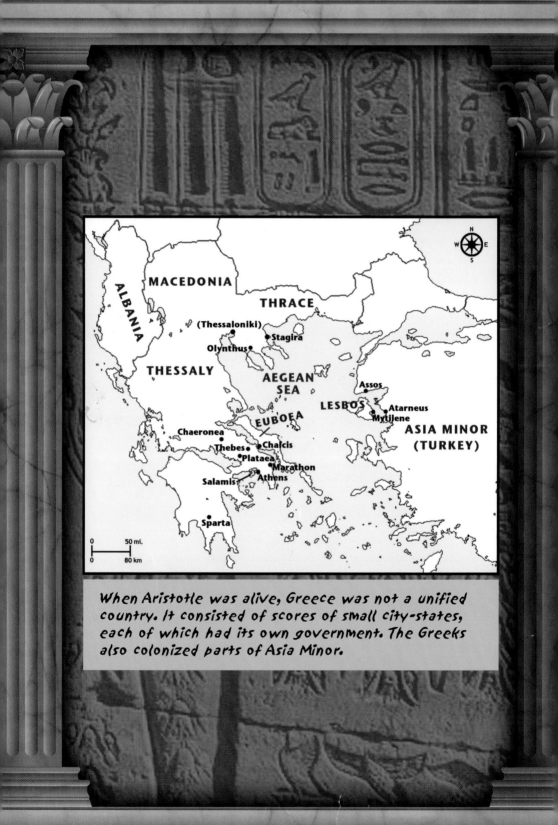

When Aristotle was alive, Greece was not a unified country. It consisted of scores of small city-states, each of which had its own government. The Greeks also colonized parts of Asia Minor.

CHAPTER
TWO

LEARNING TO THINK FOR HIMSELF

Aristotle was born in 384 BCE in Stagira. The town was in Thrace, a Greek province at the northern end of the Aegean Sea. Stagira was located about 40 miles east of the modern city of Thessaloniki, Greece's second-largest city.

His mother was Phaestis. She had come from a powerful and important family in the town of Chalcis on the island of Euboea. His father, Nicomachus, was the official physician to the king of Macedonia, Amyntas II. Physicians normally trained their sons to take over for them. It is likely that Aristotle was descended from a long line of medical people.

By the time Nicomachus became a physician, an important change had occurred in the Greek approach to medicine. For generations, Greeks (along with other people in the ancient world) believed that diseases and sickness were brought on by the will of the gods. Then a Greek doctor named Hippocrates took a completely different approach. Hippocrates looked for natural causes for illnesses. Looking for natural causes involved close examination of conditions in the real world. It is likely that Nicomachus was influenced by this attitude. He probably passed it on to his son. Years later, close observation of nature would become important to how Aristotle formulated his ideas.

Aristotle must have grown up in relative comfort because of his father's position at the Macedonian court. When he was about ten, both of his parents died. A man named Proxenus, probably a relative, became his guardian.

Aristotle was lucky. Proxenus treated him like his own son, and he recognized that Aristotle was especially intelligent. He also figured out that the tutors in Macedonia had little to offer the boy. Proxenus wanted Aristotle to have the best possible education, so he sent him to Athens. The city was the intellectual center of the Greek world. In turn, the intellectual center of Athens was the Academy. It had been founded by Plato two years before Aristotle was born. Plato had been a pupil of the legendary Socrates. Now Plato was the most famous philosopher and teacher in Greece.

Scholars consider the Academy to be the first university in the Western world. Like present-day universities, it had a relatively large campus. There were buildings for lectures and open areas where students and teachers could converse for long periods of time. There was even a *gymnasion*. This was an area where people could work out: run, box, wrestle, throw the javelin and discus, and more. *Gymnasion* is based on a root that means "naked." Plato, Aristotle, and everyone else who attended the Academy didn't wear any clothes during their workouts.

Besides the clothing issue, there were many other differences from today's universities. Students weren't graded. They never had to study for tests. They didn't receive a degree when they "graduated." The dividing line between students and teachers wasn't as sharp as it is today. As professor Rubenstein notes, "After an initiation period, a student with Aristotle's talent would be treated as an equal by scholars many years his senior; eventually, he would be invited to lead discussions and to write treatises of his own."[1]

Another difference was that there were no "professional students" who idled away their time because they didn't want to be a part of the "real world." Plato's aim was to prepare young men to become good leaders. The best way of doing that, he maintained, was to teach them to think well and to express their thinking clearly and forcefully.

Plato didn't charge any money for students to attend the Academy, but that didn't mean it was open to anyone. Most people in Athens had to work hard for a living. There was no time left for studying. The ones who had plenty of free time were mostly aristocrats. That was fine with Plato. He didn't want to educate common men.

The Academy's reputation had spread through much of the ancient world. It wasn't unusual for someone to travel as far as Aristotle had. Many students had come from even farther away.

Plato founded the school during a turbulent era. At that time, there wasn't a unified country known as Greece. Rather, what we now call Greece consisted of scores of poleis, or city-states. Each polis consisted of a central town and the surrounding countryside. Much of the countryside was farmland. The farmland helped the polis to be self-supporting.

The poleis had several things in common. Their inhabitants spoke and wrote Greek. They worshiped the same major gods. Nearly every polis participated in the Olympic Games. The Games were so important that the Greek calendar was organized into Olympiads. These were the four-year intervals between Games.

The Greeks had a hard time getting along with one another. Wars among the poleis were common. At one point they came together to defeat a serious threat from the Persian Empire (an area that included much of the Middle East). Though outnumbered, the Greeks used superior strategy and tactics to win three decisive battles. The first came near the village of Marathon in 490 BCE. The second was a naval battle at Salamis in 480 BCE. The final triumph was a land battle at Plataea in 479 BCE. The victories ensured that the Greeks would remain free from foreign domination. They could continue to develop according to their own laws and principles.

The poleis went back to their bickering as soon as the Persian War was over. The two leading poleis were Athens and Sparta. The Spartans had the best army among the poleis. The Athenian strength was its navy. The two had several conflicts after defeating the Persians. Major fighting broke out between Athens and Sparta in 431 BCE in a conflict known as the Peloponnesian War. Many other poleis became involved. Some were allied with Athens, and others supported Sparta. It was like a world war in miniature. Plato, who probably was born in 427 BCE, grew up under the cloud of this war.

As the Peloponnesian War dragged on, the Athenians suffered significant reversals. In 414 BCE they lost nearly all of their army and navy at Syracuse on the island of Sicily. The citizens began pointing fingers at each other. The city's democratic government was overthrown briefly in 411 BCE.

It is likely that by then—or soon afterward—Plato met Socrates. Socrates was one of a number of men who taught philosophy in Athens. Many people regarded him as the city's best philosophy teacher. Philosophy was important to the Athenians, because they believed that philosophy could tell them the best way to act.

Not everyone in the city approved of Socrates. He didn't think very highly of democratic government, and he wasn't afraid of expressing his thoughts. He passed his attitude on to his students.

The Peloponnesian War ended in 404 BCE. Athens was defeated. The democratic government was overthrown again, and a group of thirty men came to power. Some of the democratic leaders were killed. Others were forced into exile. The rule of the Thirty, as they were known, quickly became far too harsh. Within a year the ousted democratic leaders had regained control. They wanted revenge. So did many other Athenians. Even though he hadn't supported the Thirty, Socrates was a high-profile target.

Their opportunity came in 399 BCE. Three men brought two serious charges against Socrates: impiety (disrespect for the gods) and corrupting the youth of Athens. These charges were punishable by death.

Socrates was found guilty and received the death sentence. He was ordered to drink a cup of hemlock, a deadly poison.

Plato was shocked and horrified. Socrates' death completely turned him against democracy. To make sure that the name and ideas of Socrates would never die out, he wrote a series of dialogues. In most of the dialogues, Socrates is the main character. He has discussions with prominent citizens of Athens. He asks the citizens for their opinions about different issues: politics, ethics, the nature of beauty, the nature of love, and so on. He acts as if he knows nothing about these issues. He asks the citizens a series of questions to pinpoint their opinions. The answers to these questions show the citizens how their opinions are mistaken. Sometimes Socrates supplies a better answer. Sometimes he doesn't.

When he began writing his dialogues, Plato was still very influenced by Socrates. As the years went by, Plato became more confident in his own opinions. It's likely that in the later dialogues, Socrates became something of a mouthpiece for Plato's own thinking.

By the time Aristotle arrived in Athens, Plato was highly regarded. At home, Aristotle had been a big fish in a small pond. When he arrived at the Academy, he was a very small fish in a very big pond. At first he probably felt self-conscious and timid. He was just seventeen.

He also knew that most other Greeks considered Macedonia, his homeland, as a backward area. Many didn't even consider it part of Greece. When Macedonian athletes wanted to take part in the Olympics, they weren't allowed to. Greek athletes from "genuine" poleis refused to compete with "barbarians." To the Greeks, barbarians weren't primitive people. Rather, their languages sounded like "bar-bar-bar." Even though the Macedonians spoke a form of Greek, most other Greeks couldn't understand their dialect.

It didn't take long for Aristotle to overcome his initial limitations. He demonstrated that he was smart—very smart indeed. Many students, like some students today, had to be pushed to do their studies. Aristotle was the opposite. If anything, he was too eager. Plato often had to curb his enthusiasm. According to reports, Plato eventually referred to him as "The Brain."

Aristotle began his scholarly career greatly under the influence of Plato. Soon he began developing his own ideas. Because of his medical training, he emphasized the importance of the senses. To him, what he could see, feel, touch, taste, and hear was most real. He would go out into the world and use all or most of his senses to observe what was there.

Plato disagreed with that notion. He thought that what the senses registered were imperfect copies of ideal Forms. One of the purposes of philosophy was to learn how to get closer to those Forms. The Forms were what was most real. The best way of learning about the Forms was to think about them. Plato preferred long hours of study. To him, knowing the real world wasn't very important. This thinking was reflected in his political beliefs. The only good rulers would be men who had studied for many years. Their studies would allow them to know what was best for everyone else.

Many centuries later, Renaissance painter Raphael illustrated the primary difference between the two men. In his painting *The School of Athens*, Plato and Aristotle stand next to each other. Plato gestures upward, toward heaven. Aristotle points downward. He is emphasizing the earth as we know it.

In spite of this disagreement, they got along well and admired each other. As many people would say today, "They agreed to disagree."

Aristotle stayed at the Academy for twenty years. In 347 BCE, Plato died. By that time, Aristotle was one of the most respected teachers in the school. He may have believed that he would be appointed as Plato's successor. That didn't happen. Plato's nephew Speusippus took over the Academy.

Aristotle left Athens. He may have been unhappy that he was passed over for the position. There could have been another reason. The Macedonian king, Amyntas, died in 359. His nephew Philip succeeded him. Philip was ambitious. He began making wars against his immediate neighbors, and he won nearly all of them. His power started to grow.

For the Greeks, contempt was turning to concern. An Athenian statesman named Demosthenes began delivering what became known as Philippics. These were speeches intended to raise the alarm about the threat that Philip posed. Macedonia may have seemed far away to the Athenians, but Demosthenes believed that the city would eventually find itself in Philip's crosshairs.

His views acquired greater urgency in 348 BCE. Philip conquered the northern Greek city-state of Olynthus. He destroyed the city and sold the inhabitants into slavery.

An anti-Macedonian sentiment swept through Athens. Despite his long residency in Athens, Aristotle remained very closely identified with Macedonia. He may have feared for his safety. That could explain why he felt like getting out of town.

There could have been still another reason. While Plato was alive, Aristotle remained loyal to his teacher. He even delivered a highly flattering speech at Plato's funeral. Yet he may have felt that he had to leave Athens to develop his own ideas. At the Academy, he would have been constantly reminded about his master.

Aristotle went to the city of Atarneus, located in the northwest corner of modern-day Turkey. Hermias, the ruler of Atarneus, had attended the Academy and was a good friend of Aristotle's. He welcomed Aristotle with open arms. He gave Aristotle and his friend Xenocrates—another former Academy student—all they needed to set up a school similar to the Academy. They founded it in the nearby town of Assos.

He also gave Aristotle his niece Pythias to wed. They had a daughter, who was also named Pythias.

In his book *Politics*, Aristotle writes, "Women should therefore marry about the age of 18, and men at 37 or thereabouts."[2] He would have been "37 or thereabouts" at the time he moved to Assos. If he followed his own prescription, Pythias likely would have been 18. We don't know much about their home life. Greek wives typically spent most of their time indoors. Their main responsibilities were to maintain the household and to produce children—preferably male children.

Aristotle didn't stay very long at Assos. In 345 BCE or early the following year, he moved to the nearby island of Lesbos, the home of Theophrastus, his best student. He settled in the town's main city, Mytilene. Again he set up a school. It was similar to the one on Assos.

By this time, he had become especially interested in biology. He spent countless hours in a large lagoon near Mytilene. It contained a vast variety of living creatures. He eagerly studied them and their life cycles. It was a wonderful time. Aristotle seemed to have everything going for him: a good marriage, a fulfilling career, and the respect of many people.

This ideal life was about to undergo a momentous change.

Hippocrates

According to legend, Hippocrates was directly descended from Asclepius, the Greek god of medicine. Actually, he did come from a long line of doctors. Other than that, scholars know very little about his life. He was probably born about 460 BCE on Cos, an island a few miles off the southwestern coast of modern-day Turkey.

At the time, virtually everyone in the ancient world believed that illness and serious wounds were the result of offending the gods. For centuries, sick people went to *Asclepia*. These were religious healing centers where people would spend the night. They believed Asclepius would visit them in a dream, and when they awoke the next morning, they would be cured.

Hippocrates was born into an era when these attitudes were changing. Greek thinkers were looking for natural explanations of the world around them. Hippocrates put the practice of medicine on a natural footing. He carefully examined his patients, then made a prescription for their ailments based on real-world conditions.

Hippocrates

His methods became very popular. He trained many other doctors. When he died (perhaps in 377 BCE), he left behind more than 60 books—written either by him or by his followers—now known as the *Hippocratic Collection*. These contained descriptions of the ways in which he worked and actual case studies. He is most famous for the Hippocratic Oath. It is a code of medical ethics, which includes, "First, do no harm." Even in the twenty-first century, many doctors take the oath—or a modern version of the oath—before they begin their medical careers.

He believed that there were four important humors, or fluids, in the human body. These were yellow bile, black bile, blood, and phlegm. When all four humors were in balance, people were healthy. When they weren't, sickness was the result. One method of restoring balance was to bleed a person. The physician would open a blood vessel and allow blood to drain out.

That theory has been discredited. However, much of what Hippocrates believed was important for health is still prescribed. This includes getting plenty of sleep, a proper diet, and moderate exercise.

Alexander the Great was one of the world's greatest military leaders. Starting at the age of 20, he eventually conquered an empire of more than 2 million square miles. He died at the age of 35.

CHAPTER
THREE

TEACHING A FUTURE WORLD LEADER

In 343 BCE, King Philip asked Aristotle to come to Macedonia and tutor his thirteen-year-old son, Alexander. Philip knew how the rest of the Greeks felt about him. On one hand, they feared his steadily growing power. On the other hand, they still regarded him as a crude barbarian.

Philip wanted to make sure that Alexander learned the importance of Greek culture. He hoped that this type of education would make his son more respected in Greece. It was already apparent that Alexander was no ordinary teen. Even at that age, he was demonstrating some of the qualities that would catapult him to historical immortality.

Philip was aware of Aristotle's reputation. It probably also helped that Aristotle had spent his youth at the Macedonian court. Since he and Philip were about the same age, it is probable that the two men were already acquainted with each other.

From Aristotle's point of view, moving to Macedonia must have made perfect sense. He had developed definite ideas about the best way to govern. At thirteen, Alexander was still young enough to be influenced by a good teacher. It was clear that he was destined to rule a relatively large kingdom. Aristotle may have believed that he could honor the memory of his own teacher by teaching this young man about good government.

There was another incentive. The job paid well. Very well. Philip's generosity extended beyond making Aristotle a wealthy man. Several years earlier Philip had destroyed Stagira, Aristotle's hometown. When Aristotle accepted the job, Philip rebuilt the city and allowed its former inhabitants to return.

Greek education at that time focused on works by the epic poet Homer. Aristotle composed special editions of Homer's *Iliad* and *Odyssey* for Alexander to read and study. According to the ancient historian Plutarch, Alexander became "a great lover of all kinds of learning and reading . . . he constantly laid Homer's *Iliad* . . . with his dagger under his pillow, declaring that he esteemed it a perfect portable treasury of all military virtue and knowledge."[1]

Aristotle's instruction also included talks on morality, government, and other important topics. He seems to have had another goal. He wanted to convince Alexander that he was fortunate to be Greek. He wrote, "Europeans, as well as peoples who live in cold climates generally, are full of spirit but somewhat lacking in intelligence and skill. . . . Asians, on the other hand, though intelligent and skilled by nature, lack spirit and so are always subject to defeat and slavery. The race of the Greeks, however, which occupies the center of the earth, shares the best attributes of West and East, being both spirited and intelligent. Thus does this race enjoy both freedom and stable political institutions and continue to be capable of ruling all humanity."[2]

Scholars disagree about how much Aristotle contributed to Alexander's development. According to Plutarch, there was one area in which he was very successful. "It was to Aristotle that [Alexander] owed the inclination he had, not to the theory only, but likewise to the practice of the art of medicine," he wrote. "For when any of his friends were sick, he would often prescribe them their course of diet, and medicines proper to their disease."[3]

This famous 1653 painting by Rembrandt is entitled Aristotle Contemplating the Bust of Homer. *The clothing that Aristotle is wearing is typical of Rembrandt's era, rather than of ancient Greece.*

In fact, Plutarch continues, "For a while [Alexander] loved and cherished Aristotle no less . . . than if he had been his father, giving this reason for it, that as he had received life from his father, so [Aristotle] had taught him to live well."[4]

It is likely that Aristotle was most active during his first three years at the Macedonian court. When Alexander was sixteen, Philip left on a military expedition. Alexander remained behind. He served as ruler in place of the king. The time for lessons would have been dramatically reduced. Aristotle most likely returned to his hometown of Stagira not long afterward. His wife may have died by this time—the details are unknown. Aristotle began living with a woman named Herphyllis. The couple eventually had a son named Nicomachus. The boy was named after Aristotle's father.

Plutarch was a famous historian who was born about 46 CE in Greece. He is best noted for his Lives. *These are biographies of notable Greeks and Romans. Plutarch died some time after 119 CE.*

In 338 BCE, Demosthenes' dire warnings came true. Philips's army decisively defeated a united Greek army at Chaeronea. His victory marked the end of the independence of the Greek poleis.

Philip was assassinated two years later. Alexander became king. He was only twenty. Soon he left Macedon and began the series of conquests that would establish an empire of more than two million square miles. These conquests would make him known ever afterward as Alexander the Great. Before he left, he wanted to make sure that the Greeks wouldn't take advantage of his absence. He made an example of the ancient polis of Thebes, which had been especially rebellious against him. He tore down the city. Then he massacred the inhabitants. The other Greeks were horrified, but there was nothing they could do. Alexander left behind enough troops to make sure that no other polis would try to revolt.

Aristotle and Alexander would never see each other again.

Why Alexander Almost Didn't Become "The Great"

In 337 BCE, Philip was preparing for even more conquests. He planned to attack the Greek colonies in Asia Minor (modern-day Turkey) and add them to his steadily growing empire. Before leaving, he married Cleopatra (Eurydice in some sources), who was the daughter of a Macedonian nobleman.

It didn't matter that Philip was already married to Olympias, Alexander's mother. She was from a province in modern-day Albania. By Greek standards, that province was even more barbaric than Macedonia.

According to ancient historian Plutarch, Olympias was "a woman of a jealous and implacable temper."[5] Olympias didn't like the idea of a new wife for Philip. She tried to turn Alexander against his father. It probably didn't take much effort.

Plutarch continues, "At the wedding of Cleopatra, whom Philip fell in love with and married, she being much too young for him, her uncle Attalus in his drink desired the Macedonians would implore the gods to give them a lawful successor to the kingdom by his niece."[6]

That was too much for Alexander. He was already fuming at what he considered the betrayal of his mother. Now Attalus wanted the wedding to produce a "lawful successor"—that is, a new prince who was fully Macedonian. If that happened, Alexander could become excess baggage.

Alexander yelled an insult at Attalus, then hurled a heavy drinking cup at his head. Then it was Philip's turn to become furious. Now it was Alexander, he thought, trying to ruin his wedding feast. He was so angry, he wanted to kill his son. He leaped to his feet and pulled his sword. In his drunkenness, he fell down almost immediately.

Alexander stood over his fallen father and mocked him. He said that the man who wanted to travel hundreds of miles at the head of an army couldn't even cover a few feet in his own palace.

Alexander and Olympias fled the court. One of Philip's trusted advisers calmed down the king. He soon recalled Alexander. But Alexander felt uneasy. His security wasn't helped when Cleopatra gave birth to a son named Caranus.

His problem was solved when Philip was assassinated in 336. Alexander became king. One of his first acts was to kill the baby Caranus.

Plato (center, left) and Aristotle are the central figures in Raphael's painting "The School of Athens." Plato gestures upward while Aristotle points toward the earth. The painting also includes many of Athens' other important thinkers.

CHAPTER

FOUR

RIVAL SCHOOLS

In 335 BCE, Aristotle went back to Athens. Speusippus had died a few years earlier. Aristotle's friend and former colleague Xenocrates had been appointed to replace Speusippus. Xenocrates may have offered Aristotle the chance to join him at the Academy. If he did, Aristotle turned him down. It may have been too hard to work under someone who had once been his assistant.

Aristotle decided to start his own school. He called it the Lyceum. The school taught many subjects. In the mornings Aristotle would give fairly technical lectures for his students. In the afternoons he'd give additional lectures. These were intended for the general public. The Lyceum included what scholars believe was the first library in the Western world. And the Lyceum wasn't just dedicated to the life of the mind. Like the Academy, it also had a *gymnasion*.

Not much is known about the relationship between the Lyceum and the Academy. Apparently there were plenty of students to go around. That situation remained true after the deaths of their respective founders. Both institutions lasted into the sixth century CE.

For nearly a decade after founding the Lyceum, Aristotle's life went smoothly. He was happy. His school was prospering. He was well respected. He did most of his writing during this time, though scholars observe that many of his books seem somewhat unfinished. They speculate that the books were actually notes for the lectures he delivered. For example, theater professor Francis Fergusson comments that Aristotle's *Poetics* "is incomplete, repetitious in spots and badly organized."[1]

Philosophy professor Lindsay Judson offers another viewpoint: "An advantage of the fact that Aristotle's surviving writings are lecture notes and research papers is that you actually see him thinking aloud, worrying about problems, trying out explanations, trying to sort out why other explanations that other people have given are no good. So you actually see a great mind at work."[2]

The primary "work" that this "great mind" produced was the division of knowledge into many different categories. Before his time, the Greeks believed that all knowledge was one and the same. It could be reduced to a single set of principles.

Aristotle took a different point of view. There were many different branches of knowledge. He set up a system to classify these different branches. We still use the same names that Aristotle devised: Logic. Ethics. Politics. Biology. Astronomy. And many more. He wrote extensively about each branch.

Take logic. Logic is the way that people should think, by putting their ideas into a consistent order. Aristotle is most famous for his system of deductive logic. Deductive logic is based on what he called the syllogism. A syllogism consists of three things: a major premise, a minor premise, and a conclusion that follows logically from the two premises. For example, one might say, "All men are mortal." This is the major premise. Then one would say, "Aristotle is a man." This is the minor premise. The conclusion, which follows logically, is "Aristotle is mortal."

Aristotle also wrote about another type of logic called inductive logic. Some things are observed to happen all the time (repeatedly). For example, apples repeatedly fall downward from trees. They don't fall up. A person will "induce" that apples always fall downward from trees.

This inductive process is still the fundamental principle of science. Scientists begin with a theory to explain something in nature. They conduct research and experiments. Sometimes the evidence supports their theory. Sometimes it doesn't—at which point they have to rethink their theory.

Aristotle was also concerned about ethics. Ethics refers to the way that people should act. The Ten Commandments, from the Old Testament of the Bible, are probably the most famous statement of ethics.

Aristotle's most noted book about ethics is the *Nicomachean Ethics*. It is named for his son, Nicomachus. At the time Aristotle wrote the book, Nicomachus was relatively young. Soon he would be a young man. Like other young men, he would want to know how to live the "good life." To Aristotle, this "good life" wasn't based just on money, fame, or a successful career. He knew these outward achievements were often necessary to enjoy a good life. But there was more. He believed that everything had a purpose. The "purpose" of a human being was to act in accord with virtue and reason. As he states in the first line of the *Nicomachean Ethics*, "Every art and every inquiry, and similarly every action and pursuit, is thought to aim at some good; and for this reason the good has rightly been declared to be that at which all things aim."[3]

He realized that people often feel strong emotions and saw the danger when people are completely ruled by them. For example, everyone feels fear at some point. A courageous man recognizes this fear and moves beyond it. He becomes brave. A cowardly man recognizes the fear and allows himself to be controlled by his fear. A rash man goes overboard in his emotional response. He puts his life and the lives of others in jeopardy by his overly emotional behavior. Therefore, Aristotle believed in a mean, or a medium point, between two extremes.

Politics is closely related to ethics. The best government, he believed, would allow people to live according to their purpose. He studied the constitutions of more than 150 Greek poleis. His analysis concluded that there were three primary forms of government. Each had a "good" form and a "bad" form. The first was rule by a single man. The good form was a monarchy. Its leader was a king. His decisions reflected the best interests of his people. A tyranny, on the other hand, lay in the control of a tyrant. He ruled for his own benefit.

Second was concentrating power in the hands of a relatively small group of men. They were typically the largest landowners in the polis. An aristocracy, which means literally "rule by the best," was the good form. An oligarchy ("rule by the few") was to be avoided. The men in control would make decisions primarily to benefit themselves.

The third form gave control to a large group of people. Aristotle believed that a polity was the good form. A polity consisted of what we might today call the "middle class." It included all the men who owned property. Their successful landholdings provided them with enough leisure time to become familiar with the issues of the day. That way they could vote intelligently.

Like Plato, Aristotle despised democracy, the "bad" form of government by a large group. In a democracy, all the citizens had an equal voice—the free Athenian-born male citizens, that is. Women, slaves, and foreigners had no say in the government. Plato and Aristotle both thought that a democracy was unstable. The people could easily be swayed in one direction or the other. They also thought that everyone would be looking out for their own interests rather than for the good of the society in which they lived.

He believed that each of the three "good" forms had something to offer. Each level had control over certain functions of government. His ideal constitution, therefore, was mixed. His thinking is a cornerstone of the U.S. Constitution, the document under which citizens of the United States have lived for over two hundred years.

The largest portion of Aristotle's writing was scientific. It seems that his greatest passion in science was for biology, the study of living things. Much of what he learned was based on observation of animals in their natural habitats. He learned even more by dissecting many creatures. He invented a systemic classification of hundreds of different kinds of animals. In fact, he may have even been the first evolutionist. He was especially interested in trying to explain what caused the differences in animals.

Some of what he thought has been disproved by scientists who came after him. For example, his studies of astronomy convinced him that the earth was at the center of the universe. Today, of course, we believe that this isn't true.

On the other hand, he correctly believed that the earth was spherical. He demonstrated this by direct observation of partial eclipses of the moon. When those occurred, the earth would cast a shadow on the moon. The outline of the shadow was a curve.

In 326 BCE, his tranquil life suffered a blow. Alexander had been defeated in some battles. He was becoming increasingly suspicious of people around him, thinking that some of his followers were trying to overthrow him. Callisthenes, Aristotle's nephew, was one of the men Alexander suspected. He stuffed the young man into an animal cage. Then he executed him.

The city became much more dangerous for Aristotle when Alexander died of a fever three years later. Without its strong leader, the empire he had founded quickly began to crumble. The Athenians, who resented being controlled by Macedonia, rose in rebellion. Aristotle's ties to Macedonia were well known. Once again, a prominent philosopher became the object of civic displeasure.

Like Socrates, Aristotle was charged with impiety. It was somewhat of a trumped-up charge. It was based on a poem he had written and dedicated to Hermias nearly twenty years earlier.

While Aristotle was teaching Alexander, Hermias had been captured by a Persian army. He was tortured to death. Alexander honored his memory with a poem. Part of it suggested that Hermias had some "god-like" qualities. Of course, Aristotle never considered Hermias to be a god, but that didn't matter to the angry citizens of Athens. They were looking for an excuse to put him on trial. The suggestion of these god-like qualities was enough. The Athenians began planning to charge him with impiety.

Ironically, these same citizens had erected a monument to Aristotle a few years earlier. It praised Aristotle, saying that he "had served the city well . . . by all his services to the people of Athens, especially by intervening with King Philip for the purpose of promoting their interests."[4]

To Aristotle, the situation must have seemed a perfect example of the dangers of democracy. A few years before, the Athenians had honored him. Now they hated him. It also seemed like a rerun of the trial and execution of Socrates in 399 BCE. Socrates had been offered the chance to flee from Athens. He chose not to. He believed in the city's government. Running away would have shown disrespect for the government and would have been hypocritical. Aristotle wasn't an Athenian. He didn't have the same high regard for the government. He left the city before the trial could take place. He said he didn't want Athens to commit "a second crime against philosophy."[5] He didn't believe that someone should be placed on trial for his ideas.

He went to the town of Chalcis on the island of Euboea. His mother's family still had some property there. It is likely that he was bored. For more than two decades, he had traveled in the highest academic circles. People respected him and listened eagerly to his opinions. There was always something to learn. Now he was isolated in the country.

He died about a year later. The likely cause was a stomach complaint. Fortunately, his works didn't die with him.

Aristotle Influences the U.S. Constitution

Aristotle's political theory became very important soon after the American Revolution. The delegates to the Constitutional Convention in 1787 had all studied classical writers such as Plato and Aristotle. The delegates wanted to use some of these time-tested ideas as they created the new document.

Constitutional Convention of 1787

These Founding Fathers were sure about one thing. They didn't want a direct democracy. In that system, everyone would have an equal say in how the government would be run. Like Aristotle, they believed that such a system would be unstable. The people were fickle. They were constantly changing their minds. There was another problem. The Greek poleis that Aristotle knew were small enough so that this system would be practical. The new United States had millions of people. Direct democracy would be too cumbersome. On the other hand, Americans had just rebelled from a king. They didn't want to live under the rule of a single person, either.

Therefore, the framers of the Constitution set up a three-part system of government. There is the executive branch, headed by one person—an elected president. The second is a small group of people that make up Congress, which includes the Senate and the House of Representatives. Its members are also chosen by the people. The judicial branch is independent of the other two. Its task is to make sure that any new laws are consistent with the Constitution.

This arrangement sets up a system of checks and balances. No single part of the government can become too powerful. The people are not directly involved in the decision-making. Their greatest influence is in electing people who share their views to represent them. The Founding Fathers probably hoped these representatives would primarily be cultured, educated gentlemen—in other words, people like themselves.

Two very large and important groups in the new nation were excluded from voting. These were women and slaves. This exclusion was also consistent with Aristotle's thinking.

Aristotle believed that a government had to be able to change. The U.S. Constitution reflects this belief. It spells out the precise way in which it can be amended, or modified. Slaves were freed during the Civil War. They were granted the right to vote with the passage of the Fourteenth and Fifteenth Amendments soon after the war ended. Women had to wait until 1920 and the passage of the Nineteenth Amendment.

The whole
is more than
the sum of
the parts.

Aristotle
384–322 B.C.

One of Aristotle's most famous quotations. It means that an organism can't be entirely explained by what composes it. For example, a country often acts in a way that can't be explained by looking at the people who live in it. It takes on a life of its own.

CHAPTER
FIVE

ARISTOTLE'S AWESOME AFTERLIFE

Aristotle left his accumulated writings to his student Theophrastus. In a natural progression, Theophrastus succeeded Aristotle as director of the Lyceum. Twenty-five years later, Theophrastus died. His nephew Neleus took over the manuscripts. Neleus lived in a Greek city in Asia Minor. Its rulers frequently confiscated objects of value. According to a widely circulated story, Neleus hid the manuscripts in a cave to protect them. They lay untouched for two centuries.

Finally someone found them lying in the cave where Neleus had left them. The discoverer recognized their obvious importance. He sent them to Andronicus of Rhodes, who lived in Athens. He was a respected thinker. Again Aristotle's collected wisdom crossed the Aegean Sea.

Andronicus went to work. What he received consisted of numerous relatively short manuscripts. He organized them into a series of longer books. Each book dealt with a single category. All the political writings, for example, became the *Politics*. Then Andronicus published them. For several centuries, these books maintained Aristotle's reputation in the ancient world as a great thinker.

Eventually Christianity emerged as the dominant religion in the Western world. Christian thinkers were familiar with Plato. His emphasis on things beyond the senses was attractive to them. His thinking became incorporated into their emerging thought.

Aristotle didn't fare as well. Christians were willing to forgive Plato's paganism because he was useful. They couldn't do the same for Aristotle. He emphasized the real world over faith. Even more blasphemous, he said that human beings could figure out the secrets of the universe. Christian scholars believed that some parts of God's creation could never be known. It was a waste of time to even speculate about them. After a long period of decline, the Lyceum was shut down in 529 CE by the emperor Justinian. The remaining Greek scholars feared for their lives. They knew that the Christians often dealt harshly with people who didn't think the same way they did.

The scholars fled east to countries like Persia and Syria. They took the writings of Aristotle and other Greek thinkers with them. A century later, the emerging new religion of Islam became dominant in these countries. Muslim scholars translated these works into Arabic. Aristotle in particular became very popular. In 833 CE, the "House of Wisdom," a center for research and study, was established in Baghdad, which is in modern-day Iraq. The center featured Aristotle. At a time when Europe was in the grip of the Dark Ages, the leading scientific research was being carried out in the Arab world. Much of it was based on Aristotle's thinking.

Eventually Aristotle returned to Europe. In 711 CE, Islamic Moors had crossed into Spain and conquered most of the country. For several centuries, Christian scholars in Spain worked side by side with their Muslim peers. Eventually, the church changed its attitude toward Greek thinkers. Christians became as excited about "rediscovering" Aristotle as the Muslims had been several centuries earlier. Gradually the word spread beyond Spain. Leading churchmen in the rest of Europe began trying to connect Aristotle's scientific methods with Church beliefs. The most famous was Thomas Aquinas. In his book

Thomas Aquinas was born in Italy, probably in 1225. He became a priest as a young man and taught in many European cities. He died in 1274. The Catholic Church considers Aquinas to be one of its greatest thinkers.

Summa Theologica (written 1265 to 1273), he tried to work out the differences. He became one of the most honored of the church fathers. He was elevated to sainthood within half a century of his death.

The system Aquinas developed was known as Scholasticism. The Scholastics soon gave Aristotle a simple nickname: "The Philosopher." For them, no one was a better thinker than he was. Anything he wrote that didn't directly contradict the Bible was considered as absolute truth.

As a result, the church became very rigid. Centuries later, men like Galileo and Copernicus said that the earth wasn't at the center of the universe. The church attacked them. Aristotle had said that the earth *was* at the center of the universe. Therefore it had to be true. Church officials forced Galileo and Copernicus to give up their beliefs. If they didn't, they would have been executed. It was very ironic. These men and others used the same methods of observation that

Aristotle had always employed. Yet the church used Aristotle to attack them.

Eventually it became less dangerous to dispute the church. Scientific discoveries based on the same methods of direct observation pioneered by Aristotle put many of his conclusions in doubt.

One of the most important dealt with elements, the basic materials that make up everything from amoebas to elephants. Aristotle had given his prestige to a theory that already existed in his time. According to the theory, everything in nature consisted of a certain proportion of four elements: earth, air, fire, and water.

Today, we live under the notion that there are more than a hundred different elements, rather than Aristotle's original four. Each of today's elements consists of tiny submicroscopic particles called atoms. We think of the atomic theory as a relatively recent development. In fact, an early and primitive form of the theory had emerged while Aristotle was alive. Aristotle opposed it. Because of his opposition, the theory didn't reemerge for more than two thousand years. English scientist John Dalton again proposed it early in the nineteenth century. Even then, many people criticized Dalton. It took nearly a century for his atomic theory to become universally accepted.

As a result of "errors" such as these, Aristotle's role in modern thinking may be downplayed. Yet the passage of time has actually served to prove the truth of many of Aristotle's ideas. For example, he wrote: "It is good policy to aim so to shape things, by appropriate legislation, that no one gains a position of superiority by the strength of his friends or of his wealth."[1] Anyone who studies American politics knows that "friends" and "wealth" determine the outcome of many elections and political appointments, and that these outcomes are not always for the greater good. Aristotle also said: "The most important rule of all, in all types of constitution, is that provision should be made . . . to prevent the officials from being able to use their office for their own good."[2] This rule, too, is often broken in modern times.

When he was just twelve years old, John Dalton became the master of his own school. Some of the older boys tried to bully him. He overcame this difficulty to become one of the most respected scientists of the late eighteenth and early nineteenth centuries. He is especially noted for developing the atomic theory.

Politicians may take money from people in exchange for helping to pass laws that favor those people. After retiring from public office, they may also go to work for the people who gave them money. Ethics laws have been passed that try to limit these abuses of power.

In short, Aristotle had answers for many questions that we still struggle with today. We might not agree with all his answers, but we should at least consider them. Aristotle spent nearly his entire life thinking about the most important issues that humans face.

Physics professor Samuel Sambursky summarizes Aristotle's accomplishments. "No other personality in the history of science, and very few in the whole history of human culture, has had so deep and long-lasting an influence on subsequent thought."[3]

Perhaps the day will come when bright youngsters are referred to as "Aristotle" as often as they are now called "Einstein."

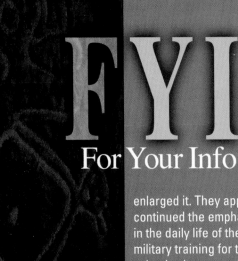

No School Today: The Lyceum Shuts Down

As was the case with Plato and the Academy, the death of Aristotle didn't mark the end of the Lyceum. The next two heads— Theophrastus and Strato—may even have enlarged it. They apparently rented additional buildings. They also continued the emphasis on science. The school remained very important in the daily life of the Athenians. The curriculum was expanded to include military training for the city's elite young men. Coupled with the city's other schools, the reputation of the Lyceum attracted scholars and students from throughout the ancient world.

It flourished under these conditions for more than two centuries. In 86 BCE, a Roman general named Sulla led an army that captured Athens. He destroyed much of the city. The destruction included most of the Lyceum. The school continued, but its influence was considerably lessened.

The Lyceum enjoyed a rebirth when Marcus Aurelius became the emperor of Rome in 161 CE. He was one of the brightest Roman emperors. He had devoted most of his life to learning all he could about philosophy and other areas of study. He provided significant amounts of money to the Lyceum and the other Athenian schools.

Athens suffered another blow in 267 CE. A tribe from northern Europe, the Heruli, captured the city. They torched many of the buildings. Again the Lyceum diminished in importance. It would never regain its former glories.

By this time, Christianity had gained importance in the Roman Empire. Many of its beliefs were in conflict with those of the Lyceum and other Greek schools. Emperor Justinian closed all the schools in 529 CE. He issued a special edict that prohibited anyone from giving philosophy lectures. The teachers at the schools realized they were in danger. They fled for their lives.

Justinian (center)

Chronology

(All Dates BCE)

384 Born in Stagira, Thrace

374 Possible death of parents; lives with Proxenus

367 Moves to Athens to attend Plato's Academy

347 Leaves Athens; settles in Assos and sets up a school; marries Pythias, who bears his daughter, Pythias

345 Moves to Mytilene on Lesbos and founds another school

343 Becomes personal tutor of Alexander the Great

340 Probably returns to Stagira and meets Herphyllis, who bears him a son, Nicomachus

335 Returns to Athens; founds Lyceum

323 Moves to the island of Euboea after the death of Alexander

322 Dies on Euboea in Chalcis

Selected Works

Categories

Eudemian Ethics

Metaphysics

Nicomachean Ethics

On the Generation of Animals

On the Heavens

On the Parts of Animals

On the Soul

Physics

Poetics

Politics

Rhetoric

Topics

Timeline in History

(All Dates BCE)

470   Greek philosopher Socrates is born.

460   Greek physician Hippocrates is born.

431   Peloponnesian War begins.

427   Greek philosopher Plato is born.

404   Peloponnesian War ends with a Spartan victory over Athens.

399   An Athenian jury convicts Socrates of impiety and sentences him to death.

386   Plato founds the Academy.

384   Athenian political leader Demosthenes is born.

382   Philip, the future king of Macedonia, is born.

377   Hippocrates dies (probable date).

359   Philip becomes king of Macedonia.

347   Plato dies.

338   Battle of Chaeronea establishes Macedonian supremacy over the rest of Greece.

336   Philip is assassinated; Alexander becomes king of Macedonia.

323   Alexander the Great dies.

322   Demosthenes dies.

300   Greek mathematician Euclid publishes *Elements*; it becomes one of the world's most respected textbooks on geometry.

264   Combat involving gladiators begins in Rome; the sport continues until 325 CE.

Chapter Notes

Chapter 1 Who's the Smartest of Them All?
1. John Randall, *Aristotle* (New York: Columbia University Press, 1960), p. 2.
2. Richard E. Rubinstein, *Aristotle's Children: How Christians, Muslims and Jews Rediscovered Ancient Wisdom and Illuminated the Dark Ages* (New York: Harcourt, 2003), p. 23.
3. Oliver Taplin, *Greek Fire: The Influence of Ancient Greece on the Modern World* (New York: Atheneum, 1989), p. 153.
4. Jonathan Barnes, "Aristotle," in *Greek Philosophers: Socrates, Plato, Aristotle* (Oxford, England: Oxford University Press, 1999), p. 197.
5. Plutarch, *Plutarch's Lives*, Volume II, translated by John Dryden, edited and revised by Arthur Hugh Clough (New York: The Modern Library, 1992), p. 144.
6. Michael Tierno, *Aristotle's Poetics for Screenwriters: Storytelling Secrets from the Greatest Mind in Western Civilization* (New York: Hyperion, 2002), p. vii.
7. Ibid., p. xviii.

Chapter 2 Learning to Think for Himself
1. Richard E. Rubinstein, *Aristotle's Children: How Christians, Muslims and Jews Rediscovered Ancient Wisdom and Illuminated the Dark Ages* (New York: Harcourt, 2003), p. 24.
2. Aristotle, *Politics*, translated by Ernest Barker (New York: Oxford University Press, 1995), p. 292.

Chapter 3 Teaching a Future World Leader
1. Plutarch, *Plutarch's Lives*, Volume II, translated by John Dryden, edited and revised by Arthur Hugh Clough (New York: The Modern Library, 1992), p. 144.

2. Thomas Cahill, *Sailing the Wine-Dark Sea: Why the Greeks Matter* (New York: Nan A. Talese, 2003), p. 129.
3. Plutarch, p. 144.
4. Ibid., pp. 144–45.
5. Ibid., p. 145.
6. Ibid.

Chapter 4 Rival Schools
1. Francis Fergusson, "Introduction," in Aristotle, *Aristotle's Poetics*, translated by S. H. Butcher (New York: Hill and Wang, 1961), p. 2.
2. Oliver Taplin, *Greek Fire: The Influence of Ancient Greece on the Modern World* (New York: Atheneum, 1989), p. 155.
3. Aristotle, "Nicomachean Ethics," translated by W. D. Ross in *The Basic Works of Aristotle*, edited and with an introduction by Richard McKeon (New York: Random House, 1941), p. 935.
4. Jonathan Barnes, "Aristotle," in *Greek Philosophers: Socrates, Plato, Aristotle* (Oxford, England: Oxford University Press, 1999), p. 202.
5. Richard E. Rubinstein, *Aristotle's Children: How Christians, Muslims and Jews Rediscovered Ancient Wisdom and Illuminated the Dark Ages* (New York: Harcourt, 2003), p. 38.

Chapter 5 Aristotle's Awesome Afterlife
1. Aristotle, *Politics*, translated by Ernest Barker (New York: Oxford University Press, 1995), p. 203.
2. Ibid., pp. 203–04.
3. Oliver Taplin, *Greek Fire: The Influence of Ancient Greece on the Modern World* (New York: Atheneum, 1989), p. 153.

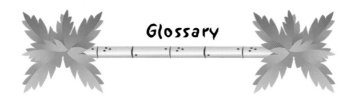

Glossary

aristocrats	(uh-RISS-tuh-kratz)—people who belong to a privileged class, often possessing great wealth and high social position.
bile	(BYLE)—a fluid associated in the ancient world with anger or depression.
catharsis	(kuh-THAR-sus)—cleansing and purification of a person's feelings as a result of seeing a play or other work of art; release of tension.
Dark Ages	Period in European history dating from the fall of the Western Roman Empire in 476 CE to about 1000; characterized by lack of knowledge and learning, and by ineffective governments.
dialogues	(DIE-uh-logz)—written works in which two or more people converse.
dire	(DIRE)—fearful, extremely urgent, potentially disastrous.
ethics	(EH-thiks)—a theory of moral principles that provides methods of determining right and wrong actions.
exile	(EGG-zile)—forced abandonment of one's homeland.
humor	(HYOO-mur)—any of the four bodily fluids (blood, yellow bile, black bile, and phlegm) that in ancient times were believed to determine a person's temperament and personality.
implacable	(im-PLAA-kuh-bull)—unchanging.
paganism	(PAY-gun-izm)—belief in several gods.
phlegm	(FLEM)—a humor that was believed to cause sluggishness in a person.
treatises	(TREE-tih-sis)—written works that follow a definite line of reasoning to arrive at a conclusion.

Further Reading

For Young Adults

Anderson, Margaret, and Karen Stephenson. *Aristotle: Philosopher and Scientist*. Berkeley Heights, NJ: Enslow Publishers, 2004.

Freeman, Charles. *The Ancient Greeks*. New York: Oxford University Press, 1994.

Jones, John Ellis. *Ancient Greece*. New York: Warwick Press, 1983.

Nardo, Don. *The Battle of Marathon*. San Diego, CA: Lucent Books, 1996.

Parker, Steve. *Aristotle and Scientific Thought*. Phildelphia: Chelsea House, 1994.

Pearson, Anne. *Eyewitness: Ancient Greece*. New York: DK Publishing, 2004.

Whiting, Jim. *The Life and Times of Hippocrates*. Hockessin, DE: Mitchell Lane Publishers, 2006.

Whiting, Jim. *The Life and Timeas of Plato*. Hockessin, DE: Mitchell Lane Publishers, 2006.

Works Consulted

Aristotle. *Aristotle's Poetics*. Translated by S. H. Butcher. New York: Hill and Wang, 1961.

———. *The Basic Works of Aristotle*. Edited and with an introduction by Richard McKeon. New York: Random House, 1941.

———. *Politics*. Translated by Ernest Barker. New York: Oxford University Press, 1995.

Barnes, Jonathan. "Aristotle." *Greek Philosophers: Socrates, Plato, Aristotle*. Oxford, England: Oxford University Press, 1999.

Cahill, Thomas. *Sailing the Wine-Dark Sea: Why the Greeks Matter*. New York: Nan A. Talese, 2003.

Fox, Robin Lane. *Alexander the Great*. New York: Penguin Books, 2004.

Plutarch. *Plutarch's Lives*. Volume II. Translated by John Dryden. Edited and revised by Arthur Hugh Clough. New York: The Modern Library, 1992.

Randall, John. *Aristotle*. New York: Columbia University Press, 1960.

Rubinstein, Richard E. *Aristotle's Children: How Christians, Muslims and Jews Rediscovered Ancient Wisdom and Illuminated the Dark Ages*. New York: Harcourt, 2003.

Taplin, Oliver. *Greek Fire: The Influence of Ancient Greece on the Modern World*. New York: Atheneum, 1989.

Tierno, Michael. *Aristotle's Poetics for Screenwriters: Storytelling Secrets from the Greatest Mind in Western Civilization*. New York: Hyperion, 2002.

Woodfin, Rupert, and Judy Groves. *Introducing Aristotle*. Cambridge, England: Icon Books, 2001.

On the Internet

Aristotle by Michael Fowler
http://galileoandeinstein.physics.virginia.edu/lectures/aristot2.html

Aristotle: A Brief Biography
http://progressiveliving.org/aristotle_biography.htm

Constitutional Rights Foundation: "Foundations of Our Constitution"
http://www.crf-usa.org/Foundation_docs/Foundation_lesson_constitution

Life of Aristotle, by Diogenes Laertes
http://www.mlahanas.de/Greeks/LaertiosAristotle.htm

The Lyceum
http://www.iep.utm.edu/l/lyceum.htm

"A Note on the Life and Work of Aristotle"
http://www.mala.bc.ca/~johnstoi/introser/aristbio.htm

Philip of Macedon Philip II of Macedon Biography
http://www.historyofmacedonia.org/AncientMacedonia/PhilipofMacedon.html

Index